Bible Crafts on a SHOESTRING BUDGET
Grades 1&2

Ellen Humbert

These pages may be copied.
Permission is granted to the buyer of this book to
photocopy student materials in this book for
use with Sunday school or Bible teaching classes.

Rainbow Publishers

Rainbow Publishers • P.O. Box 70130 • Richmond, VA 23255
www.rainbowpublishers.com

For my husband,
with love.

~ Ellen

BIBLE CRAFTS ON A SHOESTRING BUDGET: GRADES 1&2
©2006 by Rainbow Publishers, twelfth printing
ISBN 10: 0-937282-10-3
ISBN 13: 978-0-937282-10-6
Rainbow reorder# RB36128
church and ministry/ministry resources/children's ministry

Rainbow Publishers
P.O. Box 70130
Richmond, VA 23255
www.rainbowpublishers.com

Illustrator: Roger Johnson
Cover Illustrator: Terry Julien

Unless otherwise indicated, all Scripture is taken from the *King James Version* of the Bible.

Scripture marked NIV is from the *Holy Bible: New International Version* (North American Edition), ©1973, 1978, 1984 by the International Bible Society. Used by permission of Zondervan Bible Publishers.

Printed in the United States of America

INTRODUCTION

Welcome to *Bible Crafts on a Shoestring Budget for Grades 1 & 2*. Through the projects and activities in this book, the children you teach will learn more about God's Word, His Son Jesus Christ, and what it means to live as a Christian.

These Bible crafts are divided into the following categories:
- Bible Story Crafts
- Crafts About Jesus and His Teachings
- Crafts About God and His Word
- Crafts That Teach Us to Live as Christians
- Crafts for Special Occasions

Inside these chapters you will find 30 creative crafts, including puzzles, pictures, games, mobiles, story boxes, wearable art, and much, much more. Each craft has its own memory verse (from the King James Version unless otherwise noted) and teaching tips. These Bible-based projects are developed to support your teaching in Sunday school, vacation Bible school, Christian day school, Wednesday night activities, or at any other time when the Bible is being taught.

This book is intended to make every craft session fun for the teacher, too! The section labeled BEFORE CLASS gives clear instructions for any advance preparation required, WHAT YOU NEED lists all materials needed to complete the craft, and WHAT TO DO leads you step-by-step through the craft making process. The crafts reinforce Bible stories and specific Bible concepts for first and second graders, providing practical opportunities for application away from the church setting. Application suggestions and discussion starters are marked with the symbol ✱.

But more than that, these activities are a jumping-off place to get you started. Feel free to modify, elaborate, and extend the ideas presented. There are countless stories and lesson concepts for which these crafts can be adapted. The pages in this book are perforated for easy removal so that instructions and patterns may be reproduced. Inexpensive school supplies and household materials such as milk cartons, magnets, and newspaper help keep expenses to a minimum. A reproducible NOTE TO FAMILIES, requesting their help in acquiring supplies is included on page 7. Send a note home before your first craft session so parents and friends can begin gathering materials.

Children are a storehouse of creative potential. They are curious and learn best by experiencing. Given opportunities to experiment, they will blossom. In a free and open atmosphere, we promote the child. Our role is to help each one become sensitive to God's world... open to His leading. Let them try, be an encourager, rejoice with them. Work together, have fun, guide them in their walk with the Lord.

CONTENTS

MEMORY VERSE INDEX

REPRODUCIBLE NOTE
TO FAMILIES

For your convenience, the following page contains notes to families, requesting their help in collecting the materials necessary to complete the crafts. Hand out these notes two or three weeks before you need the items. Specify whether items should be brought in at any time or only on a specific date. Then simply duplicate the notes, cut them apart, and send one home with each child.

To Families of First and Second Graders

We are planning many special craft activities for your child. Some of these crafts include regular household materials. We would like to ask your help in saving the items checked below for our activities:

- ☐ small artificial flowers with leaves
- ☐ beads, small wooden
- ☐ small boxes, some at least 4 x 5 x 2 inches
- ☐ burlap, dark brown or tan
- ☐ buttons
- ☐ store catalogs
- ☐ 1-inch confetti circles
- ☐ craft sticks, wide and narrow
- ☐ 1/4-inch dowel rods in 3 and 9-inch lengths
- ☐ 5/8-inch dowel rods in 8-inch lengths
- ☐ orange felt
- ☐ felt, any color
- ☐ file folders, letter or legal size
- ☐ colored foil

- ☐ fake fur
- ☐ greeting cards
- ☐ 5 x 8-inch index cards, unlined
- ☐ 12-ounce cardboard juice cans
- ☐ magazines with pictures
- ☐ small magnets
- ☐ 1/2-pound plastic margarine tubs with clear lids
- ☐ pint-size milk cartons
- ☐ very small mirrors or trims
- ☐ 6 & 9-inch white paper plates
- ☐ photographs of events in your child's life
- ☐ plastic storage bags, gallon size
- ☐ small pompons
- ☐ sandpaper, 9 x 11-inch sheets
- ☐ textured paper

Please bring the items on _____.   **Thank you for your help!**

To Families of First and Second Graders

We are planning many special craft activities for your child. Some of these crafts include regular household materials. We would like to ask your help in saving the items checked below for our activities:

- ☐ small artificial flowers with leaves
- ☐ beads, small wooden
- ☐ small boxes, some at least 4 x 5 x 2 inches
- ☐ burlap, dark brown or tan
- ☐ buttons
- ☐ store catalogs
- ☐ 1-inch confetti circles
- ☐ craft sticks, wide and narrow
- ☐ 1/4-inch dowel rods in 3 and 9-inch lengths
- ☐ 5/8-inch dowel rods in 8-inch lengths
- ☐ orange felt
- ☐ felt, any color
- ☐ file folders, letter or legal size
- ☐ colored foil

- ☐ fake fur
- ☐ greeting cards
- ☐ 5 x 8-inch index cards, unlined
- ☐ 12-ounce cardboard juice cans
- ☐ magazines with pictures
- ☐ small magnets
- ☐ 1/2-pound plastic margarine tubs with clear lids
- ☐ pint-size milk cartons
- ☐ very small mirrors or trims
- ☐ 6 & 9-inch white paper plates
- ☐ photographs of events in your child's life
- ☐ plastic storage bags, gallon size
- ☐ small pompons
- ☐ sandpaper, 9 x 11-inch sheets
- ☐ textured paper

Please bring the items on _____.   **Thank you for your help!**

The Beginning

Your class will tell the creation story again and again, "reading" the pictures in this very special book.

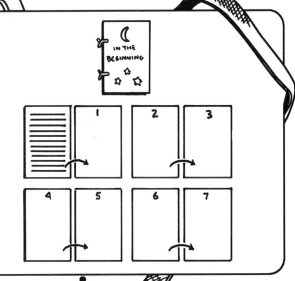

MEMORY VERSE

In the beginning God created the heaven and the earth.

— Genesis 1:1

WHAT TO DO

1. Read or tell the story of Creation (Genesis 1:1-2:3). Display a sample project.
2. Distribute writing paper. Help children read and print the memory verse from the enlarged version.
3. Let the children select a book cover and four index cards. Give them time to decorate the cover and print the title, In the Beginning, on it.
4. Help the children glue the memory verse on one of the index cards. This will be the first page in the book. Help them begin numbering the back of this card at the top with number 1. They may number the rest of the cards at the tops with numbers 2-7. The numbers indicate the days of Creation.
5. Now comes the fun. Talk about Creation, day by day. Encourage the children to share ideas and let them illustrate the pages as they talk.
6. Help the children arrange their pages inside the cover. Punch two holes through all layers, distribute yarn, ribbon, or chenille wire ties, and assist with fastening.

✱ When finished, allow time to share the books. Let volunteers take turns showing and telling from Genesis.

TIP: Temporarily slip a pencil between the yarn and the book cover while tying the knots. Make sure the book opens easily before trimming.

BEFORE CLASS

Make a large version of the memory verse. Cut lined writing paper in 3 1/2 x 5-inch pieces, one for each child. Also, cut 8-inch lengths of yarn or ribbon, two per child (or provide chenille wire).

Fold 9 x 12-inch sheets of construction paper in half, forming 9 x 6-inch book covers. Prepare a sample book to display.

WHAT YOU NEED

- ☐ enlarged copy of the memory verse
- ☐ colored 9 x 12-inch construction paper
- ☐ lined writing paper
- ☐ unlined 5 x 8-inch index cards
- ☐ colored yarn or ribbon or chenille wire
- ☐ crayons or markers
- ☐ glue
- ☐ safety scissors
- ☐ hole punch
- ☐ pencil

With the Lions

Let your class illustrate an old favorite with pen and ink. Add a frame of rocks and spend a night with the lions!

MEMORY VERSE

My God sent His angel, and He shut the mouths of the lions.

— Daniel 6:22 (NIV)

BEFORE CLASS

Duplicate a memory verse for each child. Cut two pieces of 5 1/2 x 8 1/2-inch white paper for each child. Bring a colorful selection of 9 x 12-inch construction paper sheets.

Pieces of textured papers and cardboard will be glued to these sheets to form frames of rock. Make a sample to show the class.

Bring disposable wet towels for clean up.

WHAT YOU NEED

☐ duplicated memory verse from below
☐ white paper
☐ colored construction paper
☐ variety of textured paper and cardboard
☐ ink pads (washable ink)
☐ pens or thin markers
☐ glue
☐ safety scissors
☐ wet paper towels

 ### WHAT TO DO

1. Read or tell the story of Daniel (Daniel 6:1-23). Explain that the class will illustrate this story in a special way. Show the sample.
2. Distribute practice paper, pens, and ink pads. Guide the children as they practice making fingerprints and thumbprints and add details to form animals and people.
3. Pass out paper for the picture. Help as children make fingerprints and add details.
4. When finished, let each child choose a construction paper sheet. Help the children center their pictures and glue them onto the construction paper.
5. Let the children cut out "rocks" from textured materials. Help them glue the rocks to the construction paper, overlapping the picture edge, to form a border.
6. Distribute the duplicated memory verses and read the words aloud. Let each child cut out a memory verse and glue it onto the frame.

✱ When finished, use these discussion starters or make up your own: **What if you were told to pray to the king? Would you obey? What would you do if you were in that lion's den?**

My God sent His angel, and He shut the mouths of the lions.
— Daniel 6:22 (NIV)

Noah's Boat-ful

Noah's story has always been a favorite. You can make sure every Noah has a boat-ful when you end with a surprise!

MEMORY VERSE

Noah did everything just as God commanded him.

— Genesis 6:22 (NIV)

BEFORE CLASS

Duplicate the pattern on page 12 onto white paper, one for each child. Pre-cut yarn or ribbon into 11-inch lengths and cut paper plates in half. You will need two plates per child. Now...try your hand at building an ark right along with all the other Noahs in your class.

WHAT YOU NEED

- ☐ duplicated pattern from page 12
- ☐ selection of colorful yarns or ribbons
- ☐ 6-inch paper plates, two per child
- ☐ animal crackers
- ☐ crayons or colored markers
- ☐ glue
- ☐ children's scissors
- ☐ stapler

WHAT TO DO

1. Help children cut inner portions from two plate halves. Discard the inner portions. Fasten (staple or glue) the curved edges of the outer plate portions to form a rainbow shape (see below).
2. Let the children glue pieces of yarn lengthwise along both sides of the plates to form a rainbow, trimming off the excess yarn.
3. Using two more plate halves, assist children in fastening the curved edges together to form a pocket. Attach the rainbow between the straight edges to form a handle.
4. Distribute a pattern to each child. Let the children color and cut out Noah in his boat and fold the pattern in half.
5. Let the children glue the pattern to cover both sides of the fastened plate halves.
6. Help each child cut out the memory verse. Practice saying it together as the children work. Then, let each child slip a verse into the boat.

* When finished, encourage children to help retell Noah's story (Genesis 6-9). Remember together how he obeyed God when others made fun of him. Before dismissal, slip a few animal crackers into each boat for your "Noahs" to take home and share.

Cut two

Staple

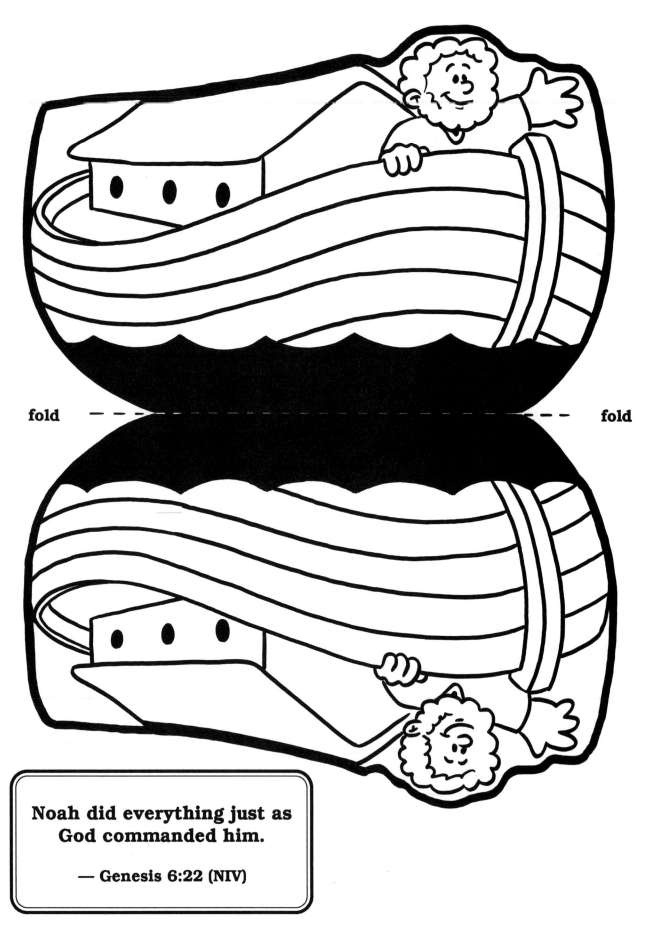

Noah did everything just as God commanded him.

— Genesis 6:22 (NIV)

Get the Picture

Like a family photo complete with sheep, this scroll sets the stage for a lesson from Genesis 37. Get the picture?

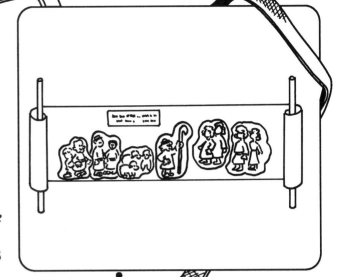

MEMORY VERSE

Now Israel loved Joseph...and he made him a coat of many colours.

— Genesis 37:3

WHAT TO DO

1. Pass out duplicated patterns, one page for each child. Let the children color and cut out the pictures. Remind them that Joseph had a special coat from his father. They may want to make it especially colorful.

2. Let the children cut out the memory verse box. Practice saying the verse together. Explain that Israel means Jacob.

3. Pass out paper strips and let the children arrange their pictures and the memory verse on it. Make sure everything fits.

4. Let the children glue the pictures and memory verse onto the paper strip, saving one inch at each end for handles.

5. When dry, help each child cover the paper strip with plastic. It may be useful to have extra helpers at this point.

6. Let children tape a straw within 1/2-inch paper folds at each end of the scroll.

7. Help each child roll the scroll to the center. Secure the scroll with a rubber band.

✱ When finished, let the children open and show their scrolls. Use this introduction or compose your own: **Picture this...Joseph wearing his beautiful coat, standing with his brothers dressed in dull shepherd's robes.** Say the verse and help recap the story as the children share.

BEFORE CLASS

Duplicate patterns on page 14 onto white paper for each child. Cut 4 1/4 x 21-inch strips of white paper, one per child. (If you use typing paper, cut sheets in half lengthwise. Tape the sheets together on both sides.)

Cut 4 x 19-inch strips of clear adhesive-backed plastic for each child (cut a few more, just in case!). Extra helpers would be useful for this project.

WHAT YOU NEED

- ☐ duplicated patterns from page 14
- ☐ rubber bands
- ☐ plastic drinking straws
- ☐ white paper
- ☐ clear adhesive-backed plastic, a 4 x 19-inch strip per child
- ☐ crayons or markers
- ☐ safety scissors
- ☐ glue
- ☐ clear tape

Now Israel loved Joseph...and he made him a coat of many colours. — Genesis 37:3

back view

Not Too Hot

Here's a red-hot idea to help you stoke up the furnace from Daniel 3. The children create their own fire.

MEMORY VERSE

Praise be to the God...Who has sent His angel and rescued His servants!
— Daniel 3:28 (NIV)

WHAT TO DO

1. Pass out the furnaces. Let children draw and color rocks on outside. Talk about the story as you work. Have the children practice saying the names: Shadrach [SHAD rak], Meshach [MEE shak], and Abednego [uh BED knee goe]. How about making your own furnace with the class? Your demonstration will help the children complete their furnaces.
2. Pass out the duplicated patterns. Let the children color and cut them out.
3. Help each child fit a pattern inside the furnace. Glue the pattern to the back half of the folded paper.
4. Use tissue paper, cellophane, and trims stapled inside the furnace to make flames shooting from the top and the door. Cover staples with tape to prevent scratching.
5. On the outside, help the children cut the door lines. Show them how to fold the door up to open. Let them glue the furnace halves together. Warn them not to glue the door shut!
6. Let the children cut out the verse. Practice saying it together. Glue it on the inside of the open furnace door.
7. Help each child tape a shower curtain hook or a paper clip on the back of the furnace for a hanger.

✱   When the crafts are finished, let the children take turns acting out the story of the three men who were ready to burn for what they believed. Let them use their own fiery furnaces as they tell it. Guaranteed...not too hot!

BEFORE CLASS

Duplicate pattern page 16 for each child.

Cut a 6 x 9-inch piece of construction paper for each child. Fold the paper in half to measure 6 x 4 1/2 inches. Place the folded edge at the side. Draw 3-inch cutting lines for a door at the bottom, one inch from each side. This will be the furnace.

WHAT YOU NEED

- ☐ duplicated patterns from page 16
- ☐ scraps of colorful tissue paper, cellophane, and shiny trims
- ☐ shower curtain hooks (or other picture hangers)
- ☐ orange or tan construction paper
- ☐ crayons or markers
- ☐ glue
- ☐ clear tape
- ☐ safety scissors

**Praise be
to the God...
Who has sent His
angel and rescued
His servants!**
— Daniel 3:28 (NIV)

A Moses-Mover

A magnet under the waves moves baby Moses across the Nile. God watched over a little basket in a big river!

MEMORY VERSE

Then she placed the child in it and put it among the reeds along the bank of the Nile.

— Exodus 2:3 (NIV)

WHAT TO DO

1. Distribute the duplicated patterns from page 18 and describe the project to the children.
2. Let the children color the river scene and Moses. As they work, read the scripture story (Exodus 1:22-2:10). Go over the memory verse.
3. Let the children cut out the river scene and the memory verse. Help them cut out Moses on the thick outer line.
4. Help the children center the river scene on poster board and glue it. Let them glue Moses on a portion of an index card, and cut it on the inner line when dry.
5. Help the children glue the memory verse in the upper left of the picture.
6. Assist the children in covering the game with adhesive-backed plastic (optional).
7. Using sticky craft glue, help each child attach a magnet to a bead. Attach another magnet to the back of Moses. NOTE: Before gluing, position magnets so attracting surfaces touch. Attach Moses and the bead to the opposite ends. The attracting surfaces should be bare.

✱ When everyone is finished, show the children how to help Moses float across river. Slide the bead underneath and watch the basket move on top. Start at the tree. Find openings in waves to reach other side. Store the game in a gallon plastic storage bag.

BEFORE CLASS

Duplicate the patterns on page 18 onto white paper for each child. Cut poster board into 9 x 9-inch squares, and cut adhesive-backed plastic into 8 1/2 x 8 1/2-inch squares, one of each per child.

A sticky craft glue is necessary for fastening the magnets.

WHAT YOU NEED

- ☐ duplicated pattern page 18 for each child
- ☐ magnets, two per child
- ☐ small wood beads, one per child
- ☐ index cards
- ☐ poster board
- ☐ gallon plastic storage bags, one per child
- ☐ crayons
- ☐ glue
- ☐ sticky craft glue
- ☐ safety scissors
- ☐ OPTIONAL: clear adhesive-backed plastic

Then she placed the child in it and put it among the reeds along the bank of the Nile.
— Exodus 2:3 (NIV)

Magnet glued to Moses game piece

Magnets positioned so attracting sides touch

Magnet glued to small wood bead

Bible Crafts On A Shoestring Budget

Prayer Journal

Encourage daily prayer, of-fering your first and second graders a very personal way to prepare to talk with God.

MEMORY VERSE

Lord, teach us to pray.

— Luke 11:1

WHAT TO DO

1. Introduce this project by reading to the class from the Bible (Luke 11:1-4).
2. Distribute copies of the memory verse and journal title. Read the words and have the children set them aside.
3. Let the children choose paper covers and fold them in half, forming 4 1/2 x 6-inch folders.
4. Help the children decorate the covers, gluing a doily or other decorative materials in place. Let them center the sticker in the design, leaving room for the journal title and the memory verse.
5. Let the children cut out the verse and the title and glue them in place.
6. Distribute the journal pages, and help the children staple them to the inside of their folder along the top. Cover the staples with tape to prevent scratching.

* When finished, read the memory verse together. Use this introduction, or make up your own: **We can talk to God any time. He's always listening. Our journals can help us remember the things we want to tell Him.**

BEFORE CLASS

Duplicate pattern page 20 onto white paper for each child. Two journal pages are provided, but more can be duplicated. Or, pages can be cut from lined writing paper.

You will need a 6 x 9 inch sheet of colored paper and one sticker per child. One 4-inch paper doily decorates the cover, or use other available materials.

WHAT YOU NEED

- ☐ duplicated patterns from page 20, one page per child
- ☐ colored construction paper
- ☐ religious stickers
- ☐ glue
- ☐ children's scissors
- ☐ stapler
- ☐ clear tape
- ☐ OPTIONAL: 4-inch paper doilies, one per child

MY PRAYER JOURNAL

Lord, teach us to pray.
— Luke 11:1

PRAY ABOUT . . .

PRAY ABOUT . . .

Gospel Glow-er

It glows in the dark...renews in the light...a gospel reminder for day and for night!

MEMORY VERSE

You are the light of the world.
— Matthew 5:14 (NIV)

WHAT TO DO

1. Distribute a duplicated pattern from page 22 and an index card to each child. Go over the memory verse. Show a completed project. Turn off the lights and see it glow!
2. Let each child cut out the pattern. Help him glue it to the center of the index card.
3. Help each child apply a coat of fluorescent paint to the light bulb. Paint over the printing on the bulb, but do not scrub.
4. While the paint dries, talk together about being a light in the world. What can children do to show others the light in their lives? Where can the Gospel Glow-er be displayed so others will see it?
5. After the paint dries, let each child turn the card over. Glue magnets to the corners. (Alternatives: Hang the card on a hook or doorknob using a loop of yarn, tape the card to display it, tack the card to a bulletin board.)

✱ When finished, say the verse together. Turn off the lights to display the Glow-er. Then, say the verse together in the dark.

BEFORE CLASS

Duplicate the pattern on page 22 onto white paper for each child. Cover the table area. You will need enough paint brushes for each child.

The fluorescent paint is available at craft or hobby stores. A small bottle (1/2 fluid ounce) is enough for approximately fifteen children. Make a sample of the finished craft to show.

WHAT YOU NEED

- ☐ duplicated pattern from page 22, one per child
- ☐ fluorescent acrylic paint
- ☐ small paint brushes
- ☐ unlined 5 x 8-inch index cards, one per child
- ☐ old newspapers (or other table covering)
- ☐ glue
- ☐ safety scissors
- ☐ small light-weight magnets, yarn, or tape

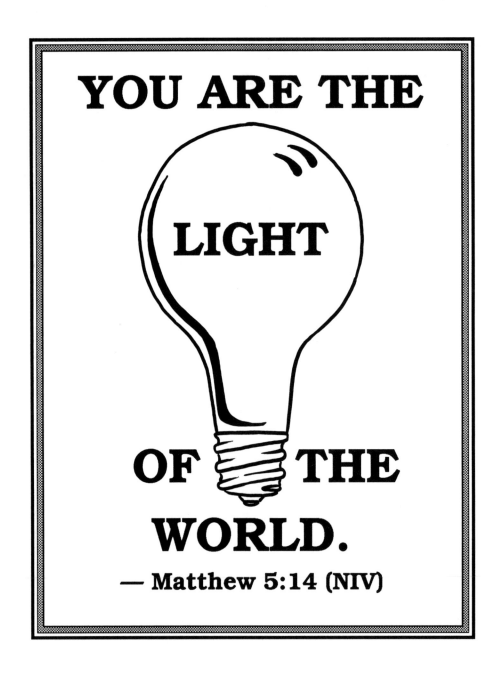

YOU ARE THE

LIGHT

OF THE

WORLD.

— Matthew 5:14 (NIV)

House Builders

Let's build a house or two! Two-sided craft stick puzzles will keep the children busy at the construction site.

MEMORY VERSE

He is like a man building a house... on rock.

— Luke 6:48 (NIV)

WHAT TO DO

1. Distribute six craft sticks to each child. Help the children line up their sticks vertically, with the edges touching.
2. Tape across the tops and bottoms of the sticks to stabilize.
3. Using markers or crayons on the craft sticks, let the children draw the house built on the rock.
4. Turn the taped sticks over. Let the children draw the house built on sand that could not weather the storm. Make sure the total surface area of the sticks is used for both pictures.
5. When complete, remove the tape and mix the sticks. Let the children put the puzzle together. Store two-sided puzzles in envelopes or wrap with rubber bands.

* When finished, give the children time to exchange sticks and try each other's puzzles.

TIP: Play a Verse Builders game to help children memorize the Bible verse. Have the children sit around a small table. Review the memory verse together several times. Designate a child to begin. That child places his hand, palm down, in the center of the table while saying the first word of the verse. Proceeding clockwise, each child takes a turn saying the next word in the verse while placing his hand on top of the previous player's hand. After everyone has his hand in the pile, the bottom hand is removed and placed on top as that player says the next word of the verse. Continue in this manner until the verse is complete. The next three children say the book, chapter, and verse. Repeat, using different children to start.

BEFORE CLASS

If you choose to use envelopes for puzzle storage, plan to print the memory verse on each envelope.

WHAT YOU NEED

- [ ] wide craft sticks, six per child
- [ ] crayons or colored markers
- [ ] masking tape
- [ ] clear tape or glue
- [ ] envelopes (letter-size or larger) or rubber bands, one per child

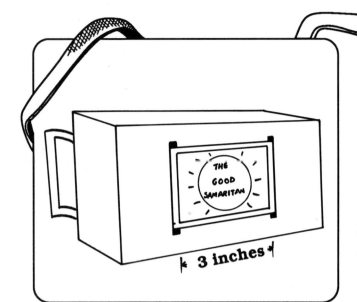

In the Movies

Here's a special film produced by the children. Lights, camera, action! Introducing...The Good Samaritan.

MEMORY VERSE

And when he saw him, he took pity on him.

— Luke 10:33 (NIV)

BEFORE CLASS

Duplicate pattern pages 25 and 26 on white paper, one of each page per child. Make two 2 1/4 to 2 1/2-inch slits in each box lid, 3 inches apart.

Provide multiple glue and tape dispensers. Make a sample movie box to display. Plan to demonstrate how it works.

WHAT YOU NEED

☐ duplicated patterns from pages 25 and 26
☐ adding machine tape 2 1/4 inches wide
☐ a small gift box at least 4 x 5 x 2 inches per child
☐ short pencils or dowel rods in 3-inch lengths
☐ crayons, markers, or pens
☐ glue
☐ rubber bands
☐ clear tape
☐ safety scissors
☐ OPTIONAL: double-sided tape

WHAT TO DO

1. Read or tell the Good Samaritan story (Luke 10:29-37). Explain the movie project. Show the sample.
2. Distribute duplicated patterns, one of each page for each child. Discuss ideas for movie scenes. Read the memory verse together.
3. Let the children draw and color movie scenes in the squares. Use lined squares for descriptions and narration. Suggest story parts and spelling if requested.
4. When finished, let the children cut out the squares and put them in order.
5. Help the children fasten the squares edge to edge on a paper strip, using double-sided tape or glue. Leave eight inches blank before and after the movie sequence. Remind the children to include the memory verse.
6. Help the children secure the edges of their pictures with clear tape folded to the back of the paper strip, as shown below.
7. Wrap the end of the paper strip around a pencil or dowel and glue. Roll it up, fasten with a rubber band, and store inside the box.

✱ Load the projector by inserting the paper strip in a slit from the back of the lid, threading it through the other slit, and pulling it from the back of the lid to move from frame to frame. When running the movie, only the lid is used. Close the box for storage.

Tape placement on strip to secure edges of squares

Woolly Wisdom

This craft will help your class learn about "shepherding" and caring for their brothers and sisters in this world.

MEMORY VERSE

Jesus said, "Take care of My sheep."
— John 21:16 (NIV)

 WHAT TO DO

1. Hand out duplicated pattern pages to the children. Say the memory verse and show the children the project samples.
2. Let each child cut out the boxes around the sheep and glue them onto index cards. When the glue dries let the child cut out the sheep.
3. Help the children glue small amounts of cotton to the sheep heads, bodies, and tails. Let them glue movable eyes in place.
4. Help the children cut ears from black felt or paper and glue them on the sheep.
5. Help each child cut strips of grass from green paper and glue the grass across the sheep's feet.
6. Let the children trace and cut a 3 1/2-inch and a 5 1/2-inch circle from light-colored paper, using the patterns you have made.
7. Let each child cut out two verses and glue one to the top half of each circle. Let him glue a sheep's body to the lower half of each circle, so the legs hang below the circle. Glue a magnet behind each circle.

✱ When the children are finished, review the memory verse. Talk about the fact that just as a shepherd cares for his sheep, Jesus cares for us. When Jesus told us to care for His sheep, He was telling us to care for each other. Discuss ways we care for each other.

 BEFORE CLASS

Duplicate pattern page 28 onto white paper for each child. You will need 3 1/2 and 5 1/2-inch circle patterns for the children to trace.

Set out the supplies ahead of time, and make a sample to show the children.

WHAT YOU NEED

☐ duplicated pattern page 28 for each child
☐ small magnets, 2 per child
☐ small movable plastic eyes, 4 per child
☐ cotton balls, 3 per child
☐ green and light colored construction paper
☐ scraps of black felt or paper
☐ unlined 5 x 8-inch index cards, 2 per child
☐ glue
☐ safety scissors

Jesus said,
"Take care of My sheep."
— John 21:16 (NIV)

Jesus said,
"Take care of My sheep."
— John 21:16 (NIV)

Out on a Limb

Children will find much in common with the little man who climbed a tree. Make a story box for Zacchaeus.

MEMORY VERSE

For the Son of Man came to seek and to save what was lost.

— Luke 19:10 (NIV)

WHAT TO DO

1. Read the story of Zacchaeus to the class (Luke 19:1-10). Hand out copies of the Bible verse and read it together.
2. Show the children the story box sample and let them choose boxes for theirs.
3. Let the children use paper to sketch their ideas.
4. Help them cut out and glue a colored paper background inside the box.
5. Let the children make other cut-outs of people and scenery and glue them in the foreground of the scene. Remind them to save a spot to glue the memory verse in the box. Demonstrate how folding, bending, extensions, and glue tabs can be used to create dimensional effects.
6. Glue the verse to an index card. Cut it out and glue it within the scene.

* When the crafts are finished, let the children take turns telling parts of the story while showing their story boxes. Practice saying the Bible verse.

> **For the Son of Man came to seek and to save what was lost.**
> **— Luke 19:10 (NIV)**

Dimensional Techniques for Paper

Glue tabs

Side extension — a folded tab glued to another piece

A piece of crumpled paper glued between two pieces

BEFORE CLASS

Duplicate the memory verse from below onto white paper for each child. Collect a variety of small boxes. (gift, check refill, etc.) You will need one per child, plus a few extras.

Stories will be glued within the boxes. Box sides form ready-made frames. Make sure each box is rigid enough to balance on its side. Make a sample.

WHAT YOU NEED

- [ ] duplicated memory verse from below
- [ ] small boxes, one per child
- [ ] colored construction paper
- [ ] unlined index cards or light cardboard
- [ ] scrap paper (for sketching plans)
- [ ] crayons or markers
- [ ] glue
- [ ] safety scissors

Ojo de Dios

Your class will enjoy this special craft from south of the border, a beautiful reminder of God's presence.

MEMORY VERSE

The eyes of the Lord are everywhere.
— Proverbs 15:3 (NIV)

BEFORE CLASS

Duplicate a memory verse from below for each child. Using a hot glue gun or craft glue, attach two craft sticks at right angles for each child. Let the sticks dry completely. Cut five to six yards of yarn for each child.

Practice the winding pattern on the craft stick framework, and make a sample to show the class. Extra helpers will keep the project running smoothly.

WHAT YOU NEED

- [ ] duplicated memory verse from below
- [ ] craft sticks, wide or narrow
- [ ] variety of thick, colorful yarns and gift ties
- [ ] shiny decorations or small mirror shapes
- [ ] hot glue gun or tacky craft glue
- [ ] safety scissors

WHAT TO DO

1. Show the sample. Explain it is a symbol used by Mexican Indians long ago, called Ojo de Dios [OH ho deh DEE ohs], meaning "eye of God." The design reminds us that God, the Creator, is the center of our lives. Say Ojo de Dios together.
2. Hand out pre-glued craft stick frames and yarn.
3. Let the children tie the yarn in a knot at the intersection of the sticks.
4. Help them wrap the yarn over one stick, around and then over that stick again, and then over the next one (see illustration below).
5. Continue wrapping yarn around the sticks, forming a diamond pattern.
6. Change colors by tying new yarn to the existing yarn length. Position knots in the back.
7. When craft sticks are almost completely covered, knot the yarn end around the stick.
8. Glue a loop of yarn to the top stick, and glue yarn tassels to the others. Glue a decoration at the center of the design and the verse at the bottom.

* Say the memory verse together. Remind the children that God is always with them.

> ### The eyes of the Lord are everywhere.
> ### — Proverbs 15:3 (NIV)

Winding pattern

Partially completed

Rebus Recipe

Here's a recipe you can whip up without ever stepping into the kitchen. A tasty introduction to this lesson!

MEMORY VERSE

Thy Word is a lamp unto my feet, and a light unto my path.

— Psalm 119:105

BEFORE CLASS

Duplicate pattern page 32 on white paper for each child.

The boys and girls may enjoy making up some of their own rebus recipes. Collect examples from children's magazines and activity books which they can look at to get them started writing their own.

WHAT YOU NEED

- ☐ duplicated pattern page 32 for each child
- ☐ letter-size envelopes, one per child
- ☐ crayons, markers, or colored pencils
- ☐ bright poster board or construction paper
- ☐ safety scissors
- ☐ tape or glue

 WHAT TO DO

1. Start your lesson by explaining to the children that they will be working on a special kind of puzzle called a rebus. Putting it together will be a new way to learn a Bible verse.
2. Distribute the duplicated pattern sheet and a piece of poster board or construction paper. Read the verse together.
3. Let the children color the puzzle pieces as they choose and glue the puzzle page onto the poster board or construction paper.
4. Guide the children in cutting out the puzzle squares.
5. Distribute envelopes. Let children attach a label.
6. Give children time to move puzzle pieces around, using the verse square as guide, until they discover the proper order. Help them as needed.

✱ Take turns reading through the sequence of squares, reinforcing the verse and helping the children understand how the pictures and symbols fit together to make words. Store puzzle pieces in labeled envelopes. Let the class brainstorm other rebus recipes.

REBUS RECIPE
(Psalm 119:105)

Thy Word is a lamp unto my feet, and a light unto my path. — Psalm 119:105	PATH	**M +** eye
lightbulb	hand **- H**	**UN + 2**
UN + 2	feet	**A**
TH + eye	**IS**	open book
lamp	**A**	**M +** eye

Words for Birds

This feathered friend up in the clouds will be a favorite with your class and will introduce a lesson from Luke.

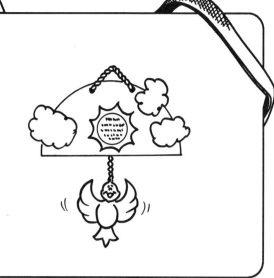

MEMORY VERSE

Consider the ravens: They do not sow or reap...yet God feeds them.
— Luke 12:24 (NIV)

WHAT TO DO

1. Introduce the lesson by showing the sample mobile. Read the memory verse.
2. Distribute two plate halves to each child. Let the children paint or color the plates blue.
3. When dry, help the children glue the curved edges of the plates together. Punch two holes centered at the top of the curve and one hole centered on the straight edge.
4. Distribute the pattern page to each child. Let the children cut out the sunshines and glue them onto the sky piece, one on each side. Let them add cotton clouds.
5. Let children cut out the birds. Help attach feathers and eyes with glue. They may use orange felt for the beaks, or color them.
6. When dry, let each child glue the birds back to back. Punch a hole at the top of the bird's head.
7. Let the children use yarn or string to make a hanger for the sky and bird. Show them how to tie one piece of yarn from the bird to the sky and another piece at the top of the sky for a hanger.

✱ While the crafts are drying (or when they are finished) talk about God's provision for all creatures. Explain that birds and flowers don't worry about anything (Luke 12:22-28). We can trust God to meet our needs, too.

BEFORE CLASS

Duplicate pattern page 34 onto yellow construction paper for each child. You will also need one paper plate cut in half for each child.

Make a sample mobile to show the children.

WHAT YOU NEED

- ☐ duplicated pattern page 34 for each child
- ☐ white paper plates, 9-inch diameter, one per child
- ☐ colorful yarn or string
- ☐ small movable plastic eyes
- ☐ colorful craft feathers
- ☐ yellow construction paper
- ☐ crayons, markers, or paint
- ☐ glue
- ☐ safety scissors
- ☐ hole punch
- ☐ OPTIONAL: orange felt and cotton balls

Puzzling Psalm

Sometimes God wants us to pay attention to our senses. This two-sided project makes biblical sense about senses!

verse side   picture side

MEMORY VERSE

Be still, and know that I am God.
— Psalm 46:10

 WHAT TO DO

1. Introduce the lesson by encouraging the children to sit quietly. Explain that you want everyone to pay attention to what happens when it's quiet. Then ask, **What did you notice?** Encourage responses that identify things God shows us through our senses.

2. Show the children the sample craft. Distribute a pattern page to each child. Say the memory verse.

3. Help the children identify their senses of sight, hearing, smell, taste, and touch. Say, **Think of favorite things each sense lets us enjoy.** Let the children draw or color their ideas in the puzzle circles on the pattern page. With smaller children, mention one sense at a time. After they draw something they enjoy seeing, have them think of something they like to hear. Continue until they have draw a picture for each sense.

4. Help each child cover the pattern page with plastic. Let the children cut on the thick rectangular outline, and then cut the rectangle into halves on the broken line.

5. Let the children glue the halves together, back to back. When dry, have them cut it into ten to twelve puzzle parts. Distribute letter-size envelopes for storage.

✱ When the puzzles are finished, practice the verse together. Allow time for working the puzzles before dismissal. Remind the children that we use our senses to see, hear, smell, taste, touch. Through these experiences we come to know God better and better.

 BEFORE CLASS

Duplicate pattern page 36 onto heavy white paper or card stock for each child. Cut 8 x 10-inch pieces of clear adhesive-backed plastic, one per child.

Make a sample craft to show the children.

 WHAT YOU NEED

☐ duplicated pattern page 36 for each child
☐ heavy white paper or card stock
☐ letter-size envelopes, one per child
☐ crayons, markers, or colored pencils
☐ clear adhesive-backed plastic
☐ glue
☐ safety scissors

Be still, and know that I am God.

— Psalm 46:10

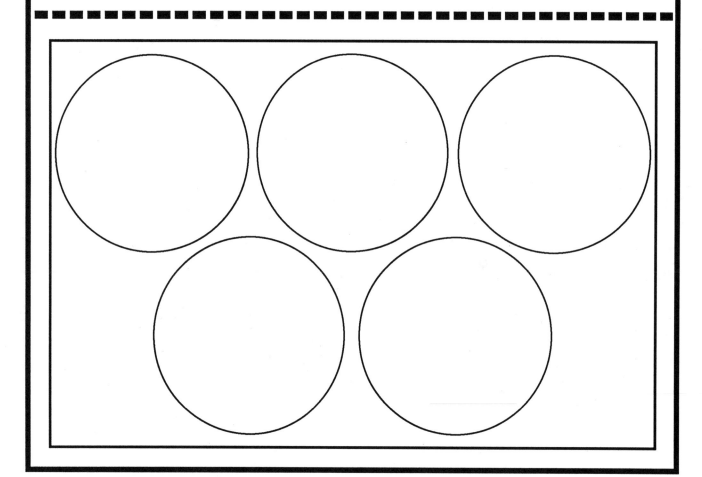

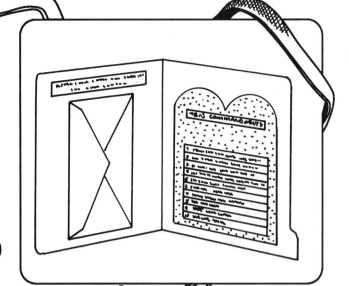

God's Rules

Long ago God gave His people rules. Today, we are God's people and He asks us to read, study, and obey.

MEMORY VERSE

And God spoke all these words.
— Exodus 20:1 (NIV)

WHAT TO DO

1. Show children the sample project. Summarize the story of Moses' meeting with God on the mountain as you distribute file folders and sandpaper tablets.
2. Let the children glue the tablet to the right side of the open file folder.
3. Distribute the pattern page. Read the memory verse and commandments together (Exodus 20:1-17).
4. Let the children cut out the verse and glue it on the left side of the open folder at the top.
5. Help them cut out the box of commandments, spread glue to cover the back of the page, and glue it to the felt. When it is completely dry, cut apart the title and commandment boxes.
6. Glue a storage envelope on the left side of the open folder. (see illustration)

✱ When crafts are finished, take turns reading commandments as everyone puts their set in order on tablets. (Hint: Rough up felt with sandpaper if it is not sticking to tablets.) Store strips in envelope before dismissal.

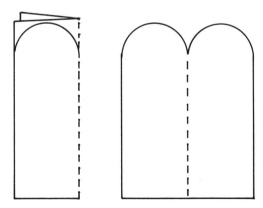

paper pattern for stone tablets

BEFORE CLASS

Duplicate pattern page 38 onto white paper for each child.

Make a tablet pattern by folding a sheet of paper in half lengthwise. Using the whole length of the folded paper, draw a rounded top of one tablet. Cut out and unfold (see illustration).

Trace the tablet pattern on the back of sandpaper and cut a sandpaper tablet for each child. Complete a sample to show.

WHAT YOU NEED

- ☐ duplicated pattern page 38 for each child
- ☐ felt, 6 x 8-inch pieces
- ☐ sandpaper, one 9 x 11-inch sheet per child
- ☐ business-size envelopes, one per child
- ☐ manila file folders, one per child
- ☐ safety scissors
- ☐ glue

> **And God spoke all these words:**
> **— Exodus 20:1 (NIV)**

TEN COMMANDMENTS

1. You shall have no other gods before me.

2. You shall not make for yourself an idol.

3. You shall not misuse the name of the Lord.

4. Remember the Sabbath day by keeping it holy.

5. Honor your father and your mother.

6. You shall not murder.

7. You shall not commit adultery.

8. You shall not steal.

9. You shall not give false testimony.

10. You shall not covet.

Footsteps Game

Follow the footsteps around a game board that your class can make as you talk about following God's Word.

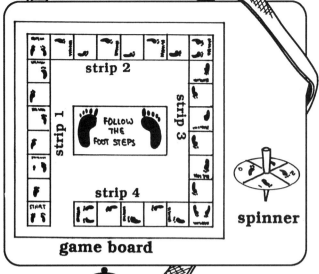

strip 2

strip 1

FOLLOW THE FOOT STEPS

strip 3

strip 4

spinner

game board

MEMORY VERSE

Direct my footsteps according to Your Word; let no sin rule over me.
— Psalm 119:133 (NIV)

WHAT TO DO

1. Distribute duplicated patterns to each child. Say the memory verse. Show the sample game.
2. Let the children cut out the game parts.
3. Give each child a piece of cardboard. Help him glue the title box in the center and glue the game strips to form a path around the outside.
4. Give each child a spinner front pattern and a 2 1/2-inch circle. Let him glue the spinner to the circle. Help him push a toothpick half through the center of the spinner to form a top.
5. When the game board is dry, turn it over to glue a storage envelope and directions in place. Pass out buttons or tokens, four per child.
6. Game boards can be covered with clear adhesive-backed plastic for durability.

✱ When finished, review the memory verse. Read the words on the footsteps and identify which follow God's Word. Go over the game rules and play in small groups. Explain that the spinner should be spun like a top, by holding the top of the toothpick, resting the other end of the toothpick on the table, and twisting. The number touching the table when the spinner stops is the number of spaces to move.

BEFORE CLASS

Duplicate pattern page 40 and the box below for each child. Provide an 8 1/2 x 11-inch or larger piece of cardboard or construction paper for each child. Cut a 2 1/4-inch paper circle (spinner back) for each child. Provide a small envelope for each child to hold spinners and tokens. Cut toothpicks in half, one half for each child.

Prepare a sample game.

WHAT YOU NEED

- ☐ duplicated pattern page 40 for each child
- ☐ lightweight cardboard or construction paper
- ☐ buttons or other tokens, 4 per child
- ☐ small envelopes
- ☐ round wood toothpicks
- ☐ glue
- ☐ safety scissors
- ☐ OPTIONAL: clear adhesive-backed plastic

FOLLOW THE FOOTSTEPS

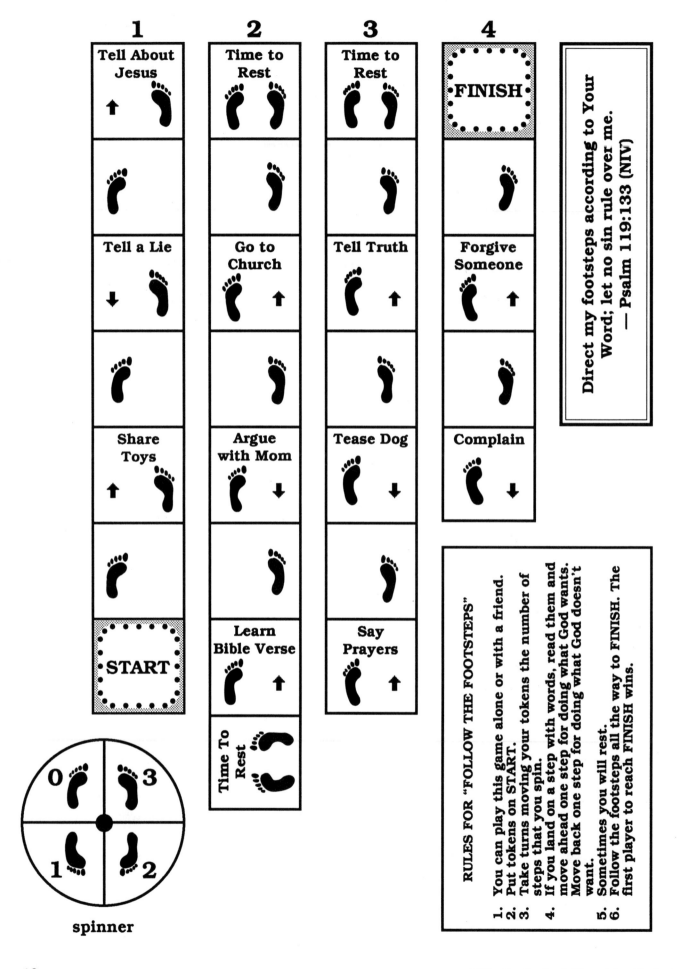

1

Tell About Jesus

Tell a Lie

Share Toys

START

2

Time to Rest

Go to Church

Argue with Mom

Learn Bible Verse

Time To Rest

3

Time to Rest

Tell Truth

Tease Dog

Say Prayers

4

FINISH

Forgive Someone

Complain

Direct my footsteps according to Your Word; let no sin rule over me.
— Psalm 119:133 (NIV)

spinner

0 3
1 2

RULES FOR "FOLLOW THE FOOTSTEPS"

1. You can play this game alone or with a friend.
2. Put tokens on START.
3. Take turns moving your tokens the number of steps that you spin.
4. If you land on a step with words, read them and move ahead one step for doing what God wants. Move back one step for doing what God doesn't want.
5. Sometimes you will rest.
6. Follow the footsteps all the way to FINISH. The first player to reach FINISH wins.

Bible Crafts On A Shoestring Budget

My Heart Chart

How important it is to memorize Scripture. Help your class make a visual record of verses they know.

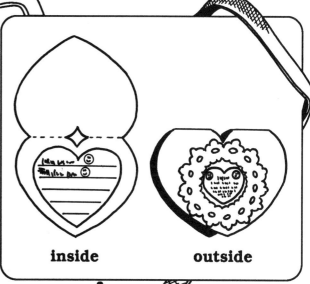

inside   outside

MEMORY VERSE

I have hidden Your Word in my heart.
— Psalm 119:11 (NIV)

WHAT TO DO

1. Show the sample. Explain that the Heart Chart is a way to keep track of the memory verses the children learn.
2. Distribute the duplicated pattern from page 42. Read the verse together. Let the children cut out the large heart pattern.
3. Let each child select colored paper. Demonstrate how to fold it in half widthwise for tracing.
4. Help the children trace and cut out a folded heart.
5. Let the children cut out the lined heart and glue it inside the folded heart.
6. Assist as needed while the children decorate the outside of the folded heart. Help them cut out the small heart verse and glue it on the folded heart.

✱ When the crafts are finished, practice saying the memory verse together. Write the children's names and the Scripture reference for the lesson on the Heart Charts (or help children write them). Explain that you will put special stickers on the charts when the children say the verse without help (or with two or three mistakes). Plan to store the hearts for them, or suggest that they bring the hearts to class each week for updating.

BEFORE CLASS

Duplicate pattern page 42 onto white paper for each child. If you have left-over supplies from other paper crafts, set them out for the boys and girls to use in decorating their Heart Charts. Make a sample to display.

WHAT YOU NEED

- ☐ duplicated pattern from page 42
- ☐ 6 x 12-inch bright construction paper for each child
- ☐ small decorative stickers
- ☐ 4-inch paper doilies
- ☐ crayons, markers, or pens
- ☐ glue
- ☐ safety scissors

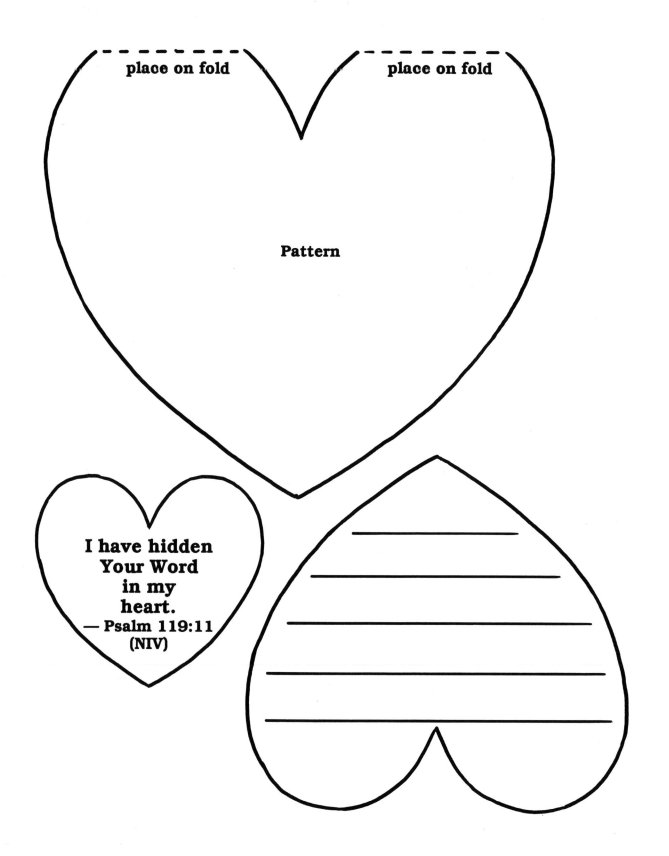

place on fold   place on fold

Pattern

I have hidden
Your Word
in my
heart.
— Psalm 119:11
(NIV)

My Lord's House

From youngest to oldest we regularly worship in God's house. A mini church proclaims this Scripture.

MEMORY VERSE

Let us go into the house of the Lord.
— Psalm 122:1

glue on paper strips

completed project

WHAT TO DO

1. Show the sample. Read the memory verse and say it together. Display the sample project where the children can see it while they work.
2. Distribute a milk carton and two paper strips to each child. Help the children glue the strips to the carton sides, starting at the ridge of the roof and working down. Show them how to gently bend the strips to match the carton shape. Finish by gluing the bottom surface.
3. Distribute a duplicated pattern page to each child. Let the children color. Windows may be colored or covered with foil.
4. Let the children color the carton roof. Help them draw side windows and color or decorate with foil.
5. Help the children cut out and glue the end pieces and the cross on the church.

✱ When the crafts are finished, discuss reasons we go to church, and what happens there. If some children do not go to church, plan time to take your class into the church before or after the service.

BEFORE CLASS

Duplicate pattern page 44 onto heavy white paper or card stock for each child. Using the same type of white paper, cut two 2 3/4 x 8-inch strips per child.

Open, wash, and dry a pint-sized milk carton for each child. Staple the cartons back into their original unopened form. Make a sample project to display.

WHAT YOU NEED

☐ duplicated pattern page 44, one per child
☐ pint-sized milk cartons, one per child
☐ heavy white construction paper or card stock
☐ crayons or markers
☐ safety scissors
☐ glue
☐ stapler
☐ OPTIONAL: colored foil

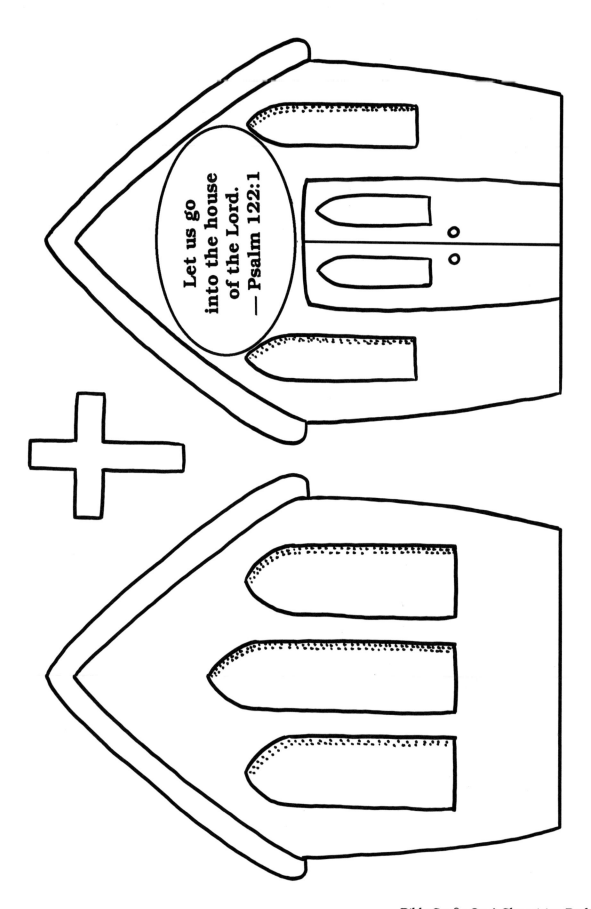

Let us go into the house of the Lord. —Psalm 122:1

Special Offering

Sharing — that's what God wants us to do. This craft encourages a personal response to God's Word.

MEMORY VERSE

Share with others, for with such sacrifices God is pleased.

— Hebrews 13:16 (NIV)

WHAT TO DO

1. Distribute a duplicated pattern page to each child. Say the verse together. Show your sample craft. Explain the reason for the special offering for which the project is made.
2. Let the children glue the pattern page onto construction paper and cut out the patterns. Cut two side patterns and tape them together.
3. Help each child arrange flowers and leaves along the construction paper length of the side pattern, leaving a 1/2-inch uncovered area at each end, and glue or tape the flowers in place. When it dries, let the child wrap it around the sides of a margarine tub and glue or tape in place.
4. Let the children wrap colored tape around the lower half of the tub, covering any stems. Smooth the tape to the underside of the tub. Glue the bottom pattern on the bottom of the tub.
5. Help the children make matching slots in the lid pattern and the plastic lid.
6. Write the name of your offering project for the children to see. Let them print it on their label and color and cut out the label and the verse box.
7. Help the children glue the label and verse to the construction paper side of the lid pattern. Help them glue the lid pattern inside the margarine tub lid so words can be seen through the plastic. The glue will be on the construction paper side. (If the lids are not clear, place the glue on the other side and glue the pattern on top of the lid.)

* When finished, review the verse. Offer children "first coins" for their Special Offerings. Discuss other ways to share of themselves for God (time, talent, being kind to others, etc.).

BEFORE CLASS

Duplicate pattern page 46 onto white paper for each child.

Trim artificial flower stems to 1 1/2-inch lengths.

Make a sample container to show the class.

WHAT YOU NEED

- ☐ duplicated pattern page 46 for each child
- ☐ colored plastic tape
- ☐ bright construction paper
- ☐ 1/2-pound plastic margarine tubs with clear lids, one per child
- ☐ small artificial flowers with leaves
- ☐ a penny or small coin for each child
- ☐ safety scissors
- ☐ pencils or pens
- ☐ glue
- ☐ clear tape

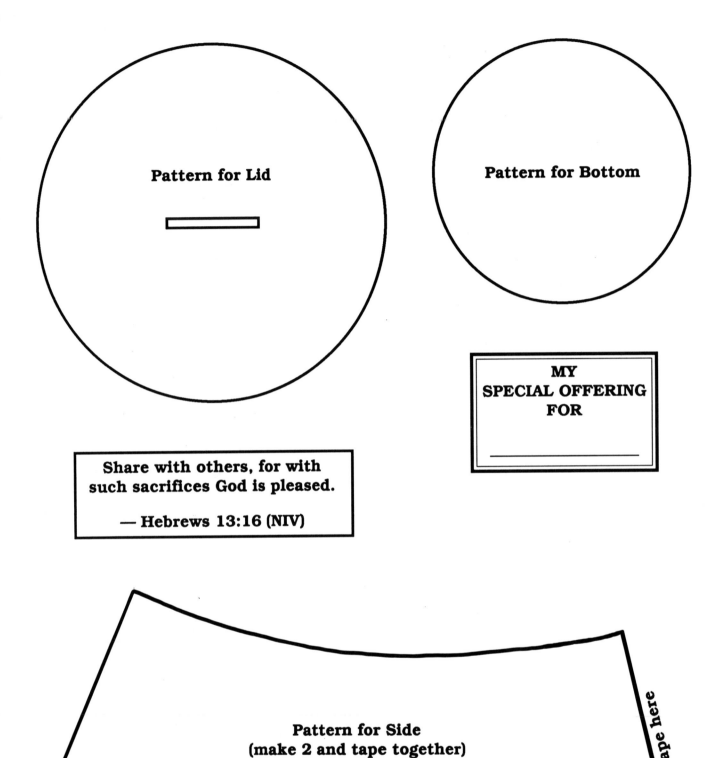

Pattern for Lid

Pattern for Bottom

**MY
SPECIAL OFFERING
FOR**
_____

Share with others, for with
such sacrifices God is pleased.

— Hebrews 13:16 (NIV)

Pattern for Side
(make 2 and tape together)

tape here

Muscle Mania

Here's a take-home Scripture reminder that will have the children flexing their memory muscles for days!

MEMORY VERSE

Be strong in the Lord, and in the power of His might.

— Ephesians 6:10

WHAT TO DO

1. Begin the lesson by showing the craft sample. Distribute a duplicated pattern page to each child. Say the memory verse.
2. Let the children cut out and fold the pattern. Help them overlap and glue the end sections, forming triangular bases.
3. Give each child two chenille wires. Help the children bend the first wire in half, twisting the top for the neck and torso, spreading wires at the bottom for legs and feet (see the illustration above).
4. Help the children bend the second wire in half. Secure this wire to the torso at arm level, twisting once around so half the wire extends on each side. Bend arms, forming elbows and hands.
5. Let the children fashion head and arm muscles and clothing from construction paper scraps and glue them on the chenille wire figure. Add fake fur or yarn for hair.
6. Help each child glue the figure to the triangular base next to the memory verse.

✱ When the figures are finished, read the memory verse together. Say, **Our memory verse tells us to be strong. Muscles are one kind of strength. How else can we be strong?** Talk about obeying God and reading/listening to His Word, the Bible.

BEFORE CLASS

Duplicate pattern page 48 on heavyweight colored construction paper for each child.

Set out a colorful selection of construction paper scraps, fake fur, and yarn. Make a sample of the craft to show.

WHAT YOU NEED

- ☐ duplicated pattern page 48 for each child
- ☐ fake fur or yarn scraps
- ☐ colorful chenille wire, 2 per child
- ☐ heavyweight colored construction paper or poster board
- ☐ construction paper scraps
- ☐ crayons or markers
- ☐ glue
- ☐ safety scissors

**Be strong
in the Lord,
and in the power
of His might.**
— Ephesians 6:10

Pencil Pals

Let's give the school year a proper sendoff with a lesson from Proverbs and a holder for pencils and pens.

MEMORY VERSE

Hold on to instruction, do not let it go.
— Proverbs 4:13 (NIV)

WHAT TO DO

1. Introduce the project by showing the children the sample. Distribute a pattern page to each child. Read the memory verse together.

2. Let each child choose a can and a felt rectangle. Help him put glue on the can surface and wrap it with felt. Explain that the felt will extend above the top of the can. Glue the overlapping end to finish.

3. Finish the top edge by helping the children cut slits in the felt, cutting from the top down to the can rim at 1-inch intervals. Spread glue along the inside top of the can. Fold the felt pieces over the top and glue down.

4. Turn the can so the seam is at back. Cut out the verse and glue it to the front of the can.

5. Let the children decorate the cans, coloring and cutting out the patterns or making their own. Help them arrange the patterns and glue them to the felt covered can.

6. Show the children how to glue several small pompons together and add movable plastic eyes to create a caterpillar. Two pompons, one with eyes, glued on top of three bent chenille wire pieces can form a spider.

* When the crafts are finished, place a new pencil in each can. Show them how to twist two chenille wires together at one end and spread slightly apart at the other to form antennae. Glue the wire to a pompon with eyes and wrap it around the eraser end of the pencil to form another caterpillar type creature. Talk about being ready to learn at school, at church, and at home. Review the memory verse once more.

BEFORE CLASS

Duplicate pattern page 50 on white paper for each child. Clean and completely dry the cardboard juice cans.

Cut colored felt into 5 x 9-inch pieces, and set out buttons, ribbon, yarn and artificial flowers.

Make a sample project.

WHAT YOU NEED

- ☐ duplicated pattern page 50, one per child
- ☐ 5 x 9-inch felt pieces
- ☐ one 12-ounce cardboard juice can per child
- ☐ colorful felt scraps
- ☐ small pompons
- ☐ buttons
- ☐ yarn and ribbon
- ☐ small silk flowers
- ☐ movable plastic eyes
- ☐ chenille wires
- ☐ new pencils
- ☐ crayons and markers
- ☐ glue
- ☐ safety scissors

Button Badges

We are all called to tell the good news, even children. Button Badges — good news to wear and share!

MEMORY VERSE

Go ye into all the world, and preach the gospel to every creature.

— Mark 16:15

WHAT TO DO

1. Show the children the sample badges. Explain that they will be making messages to wear or give to others. Button Badges can tell about God's Love, Jesus Christ, and the church.
2. Distribute a duplicated pattern page to each child. Say the verse together.
3. Let the children cut out the badges.
4. Circulate to assist as the children color and decorate the badges. Explain that blank badges are for creating their own ideas.
5. As the children work, let them suggest other badge messages that share the Gospel. Help them with spelling.
6. On each badge, help the children punch a hole through the black dot, and cut along the line from the bottom up to hole.

✱ When the crafts are finished, practice saying the verse together again. Help the children slip a verse badge over a button. (Be ready with some safety pins for children without buttons.) Allow time for the children to show the badges they've made.

BEFORE CLASS

Duplicate pattern page 52 onto heavy white paper or poster board for each child.

If you have leftover supplies, set them out for the children to use in developing their own badge ideas. You may want to cut out some blank badges ahead of time. Make a few samples to show. Plan to wear one. Better yet, wear two!

WHAT YOU NEED

- ☐ duplicated pattern page 52 for each child
- ☐ scraps of felt
- ☐ yarn, ribbon, and shiny trims
- ☐ heavy white paper or poster board
- ☐ safety pins
- ☐ crayons, markers, or pens
- ☐ safety scissors
- ☐ glue
- ☐ hole punch

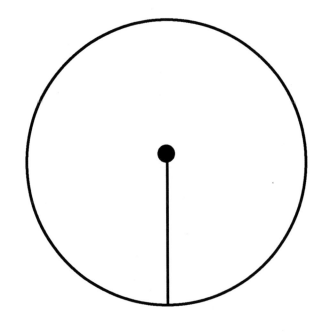

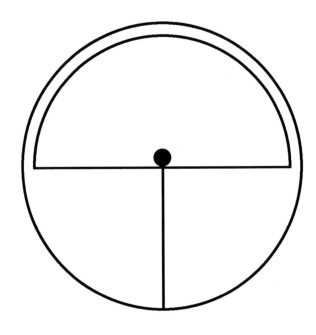

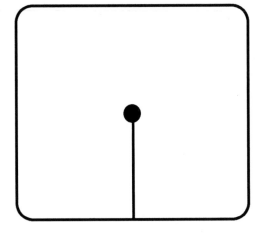

Thank-You List

Help the children celebrate a daily Thanksgiving as they create journals of thanks... banners of special blessings.

MEMORY VERSE

It is a good thing to give thanks unto the Lord.

— Psalm 92:1

WHAT TO DO

1. Give a duplicated pattern page to each child and say the Bible verse. Show the completed project. Talk about things for which they are thankful.
2. Let the children cut out the words and the memory verse and glue them onto felt, leaving a margin of material around both pieces. When dry, trim the felt, leaving a 1/2-inch felt margin visible around the edge.
3. Distribute burlap strips and dowels. Let the children spread glue at one end of the burlap, place the dowel at that end, and fold a 1 1/2-inch hem over the dowel, gluing the burlap together.
4. Help the children glue fall leaves at the top of the burlap on the front side. Below this, glue the thank you sign. At the bottom, glue the verse.
5. The rest of this project is up to each child. Have they brought items from home to glue on? Using pieces of paper, let the children write labels for the items, naming the things for which they are thankful. Mount some on felt. Then glue the items on the banner. Add more items later or provide miscellaneous craft items such as feathers, movable eyes, crayons, etc. Perhaps some photos?
6. Let each child add a hanger and streamers with yarn or ribbon. Use a touch of glue to secure knots to the dowel.

* When the crafts are finished, practice the memory verse. Let the children share their banners, explaining the various items they included. Help them name several reasons to be thankful every day.

BEFORE CLASS

Tell the class about the project in advance so they can collect items to include. Duplicate pattern page 54 on white paper for each child. Cut orange felt into 5 x 5-inch squares and cut one 3-yard length of yarn or ribbon for each child. Cut burlap into 6 x 36-inch strips for each child. Prepare a sample.

WHAT YOU NEED

- ☐ duplicated pattern from page 54
- ☐ orange felt
- ☐ burlap, dark brown or tan
- ☐ colored ribbon or yarn
- ☐ colored leaves (real, artificial, or paper)
- ☐ white paper or poster board
- ☐ 8-inch lengths of 5/8-inch dowel rods.
- ☐ crayons or markers
- ☐ glue
- ☐ safety scissors

It is a good thing to give
thanks unto the Lord.
— Psalm 92:1

54

Good News!

Proclaim the Good News of Christmas, news as important today as it was long ago. Create a banner!

MEMORY VERSE

For God so loved the world, that He gave His only begotten Son.

— John 3:16

WHAT TO DO

1. Give one newpaper page to each child. Help the children fold the paper lengthwise and glue, then fold again from top to bottom and glue, leaving a narrow unglued area at the second fold for the dowel rod (see the illustration below).

2. Help each child slip a dowel rod through the opening in the top of the newspaper.

3. Hand out a duplicated pattern page to each child. Let the children cut out and arrange the patterns on glued newspaper. Make sure the dowel rod is at the top. Let the children glue the patterns in place and glue shiny trim to the star.

4. Help each child place two 18-inch ribbons together and tie them to one end of the the dowel rod. Do the same with two more ribbons, tied to the other end of the dowel. Tie the ribbon ends together to create a hanger.

5. Tie longer ribbons to each end of the dowel as streamers. Fasten shorter curled ribbons at the center of the hanger.

* When the crafts are finished, talk together about how we get news today. Then ask, **How did people get news long ago?** Explain that they had no TV, radio, or newspapers. **What were some ways good news of Jesus was communicated?**

1

fold

2

fold

3

BEFORE CLASS

Duplicate pattern page 56 onto white paper for each child. Cut one page of newspaper (22 x 13 inches) and one 9-inch length of 1/4-inch dowel rod per child.

For hangers, cut four 18-inch lengths of ribbon per child. For end streamers, cut four to six 2 to 3-yard lengths of ribbon per child. For mid-hanger streamers, cut two or three 12-inch lengths of ribbon per child.

WHAT YOU NEED

- ☐ duplicated pattern page 56 for each child
- ☐ newspaper, one page per child
- ☐ 1/4-inch dowel rods cut into 9-inch lengths
- ☐ selection of ribbons and trims
- ☐ glue
- ☐ safety scissors

GOOD NEWS! BORN! IS

JESUS

For God so loved the world,
that He gave
His only begotten Son.

— John 3:16

Remembrance

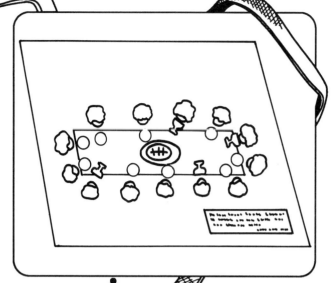

They sat together one last time...Jesus and the twelve. Create a mini-mural to celebrate that special time.

MEMORY VERSE

This do in remembrance of Me.
— I Corinthians 11:24

WHAT TO DO

1. Set the scene for this project by telling the story of the Last Supper (Mark 14:12-26). Show pictures and discuss the things Jesus said. Describe the way in which your church celebrates communion. Explain that Christians are following Jesus' example when they remember Him with communion.

2. Explain the project. Show your sample.

3. Distribute white poster paper to each child. It may help to tape it to the table until the project is completed. Let the children select paper for the table and cut it out. Position it on the poster paper.

4. Let the children select colors for people shapes and cut them out. Help them position the people around the table. Overlapping produces a nice effect.

5. Help the children design cups, plates, and bread. Let them cut out the items and position them on the table pattern.

6. Make a large copy of the memory verse and let the children copy it onto separate pieces of lined paper. Help them glue the verse onto colored paper and position it on the poster paper.

7. Help the children glue everything onto the poster paper, starting with the table, and overlapping the other pieces in succession.

8. Let each child trim excess paper from the ends of the poster paper.

* When finished, say the memory verse together. Show the mini-murals. Discuss what each shape represents. Help the children understand that celebrating communion is a way of remembering Jesus' life and teachings.

BEFORE CLASS

Bring pictures of the Last Supper and church communion vessels to class for a close look.

Print the memory verse onto a large sheet for the children to copy. Cut white poster paper into 36 x 9-inch pieces, one per child. A varied selection of paper and gift wrap will encourage creativity. Set out supplies ahead of time so children can help themselves.

WHAT YOU NEED

☐ lined writing paper
☐ colored construction paper
☐ patterned napkins and tissue
☐ scraps of foil and gift wrap
☐ white poster paper
☐ glue
☐ safety scissors
☐ crayons, markers, or pens

He Has Risen!

Like stained glass shimmering in the sunlight, a rainbow of colors celebrates the thrilling message of Easter.

MEMORY VERSE

He is not here; He has risen, just as He said.

— Matthew 28:6 (NIV)

BEFORE CLASS

Duplicate two copies of the Bible verse below onto white paper for each child. Cut strips of clear adhesive-backed plastic measuring 9 x 2 1/2 inches and 6 x 2 1/2 inches, two of each per child.

Bags of confetti are usually available at party/crafts stores. You can make your own confetti from colored tissue paper.

WHAT YOU NEED

- ☐ duplicated memory verse pattern from below
- ☐ 1-inch colored confetti circles
- ☐ clear adhesive-backed plastic
- ☐ colorful yarn or ribbon
- ☐ clear tape
- ☐ hole punch
- ☐ safety scissors

WHAT TO DO

1. Distribute strips of clear adhesive-backed plastic (2 long and 2 short) and confetti to each child.
2. Help each child peel the back off one long plastic piece and place it on the table, sticky side up.
3. Let the children cover the plastic with confetti.
4. When satisfied with the results, peel the backing from the other long piece of adhesive-backed plastic and place it over the confetti, matching the edges of the plastic. Set aside.
5. Follow the same procedure (steps 2-4) for the short pieces of plastic.
6. Tape the finished strips together to form a cross.
7. Distribute two verse circles to each child. Let the children cut them out and attach one to each side of the cross with tape or adhesive-backed plastic.
8. Punch a hole near top of the cross. Help each child tie a yarn or ribbon hanger to through it.

✱ When finished, ask the children to hold their crosses up to the light. Suggest they hang them so others can read the Easter message.

He is not here; He has risen just as He said.

—Matthew 28:6 (NIV)

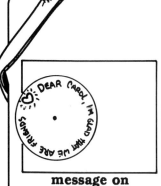

**message on
movable wheel**

Glad Greetings

Special greetings for special friends will keep your class busy as they make Valentines with movable messages!

MEMORY VERSE

A friend loves at all times.
— Proverbs 17:17 (NIV)

BEFORE CLASS

Duplicate pattern page 60 on light colored construction paper, and pattern page 61 on heavyweight white paper for each child.

Be prepared to help children think of, spell, and/or write appropriate Valentines words and messages. A large writing surface like a chalk board or tablet will be useful for writing words children can copy onto their cards. Make a sample card.

WHAT YOU NEED

- ☐ duplicated patterns from pages 60 and 61
- ☐ light colored construction paper
- ☐ heavyweight white paper or poster board
- ☐ brass paper fasteners
- ☐ crayons, markers, pens, or pencils
- ☐ safety scissors
- ☐ glue

 WHAT TO DO

1. Distribute a colored pattern page to each child and let them cut out the card pattern. Help the children cut and remove the oval by cutting an X in the center. Read the verse together.
2. Fold the card on the broken line, so the edges match and the printing is on the outside.
3. Help the children fill in the TO and FROM blanks and write a short greeting around the opening.
4. Distribute a white pattern page to each child. Use your sample to demonstrate the wheel movement inside the card. Let the children cut out the wheel.
5. Help each child attach the wheel inside the card and place a fastener through the large dots on the card front and the wheel, and through the card back. Test the wheel and trim, if necessary.
6. Let the children design and/or color several pattern decorations, cut them out, and glue them on the card.
7. Help the children write messages on the wheels, through the window, turning the wheel for more space to write.
8. Help the children glue the top corners of the card shut. Remind them not to glue the wheel.

✱ When the crafts are finished, let the children show and describe them to each other. Talk about times other than Valentine's Day when sending cards can be thoughtful. Say the memory verse together.

Cut out

TO: _____

FROM: _____

A friend loves at all times.
— Proverbs 17:17 (NIV)

- **fold**

Personal Mats

Favorite pictures, good wishes, happy memories, and thanks...all this in a special placemat gift for Mom or Dad.

MEMORY VERSE

Honor your father and your mother.
— Exodus 20:12 (NIV)

BEFORE CLASS

Help your class collect things to include in this craft. Duplicate pattern page 63 onto white paper. Cut one 9 x 14-inch cardboard piece or a side of a legal size file folder without tabs for each child. Cut two pieces of adhesive-backed plastic per child, one 11 x 16-inch and one 8 x 13-inch. Uncurl it to make it more manageable.

WHAT YOU NEED

☐ duplicated pattern page 63 for each child
☐ crayons or markers
☐ glue
☐ safety scissors
☐ lightweight cardboard or legal file folders
☐ old greeting cards, magazines, catalogs
☐ photographs and children's drawings
☐ clear adhesive-backed plastic

WHAT TO DO

1. Distribute a duplicated pattern page to each child. Let the children color one of the pictures, then cut out the picture and the verse.
2. Distribute cardboard to each child. Help the children center and glue the picture in place. Let them glue the verse in one of the corners.
3. Give children time to select, trim and place pictures or other items around the edge of the cardboard. (Some will be from home, others from magazines, catalogs and cards you have provided.) Let the children glue the pictures in place.
4. When dry, help the children peel off the backing of the larger plastic piece and place it sticky side up on a flat surface. Have them center the picture and place it on the plastic, face down, smoothing out any bubbles. Help them cut off the corners of the plastic and fold the sides to the back of the placemat. Let them place the smaller plastic piece on the back of the placemat.

✱ As the class works, encourage discussion about Mom, Dad, or another special person. Ask, **What does it mean to honor parents?** When finished, let the children show their placemats, explaining the significance of the items included for their special people.

Honor your father and your mother.

— Exodus 20:12 (NIV)